THE UNIVERSE AS PICTURED
IN
MILTON'S PARADISE LOST

An Illustrated Study for Personal and Class Use

By WILLIAM FAIRFIELD WARREN

GORDIAN PRESS,
NEW YORK
1968

Originally Published 1915

Reprinted 1968

Library of Congress Catalog Card Number — 68-59037

Published by GORDIAN PRESS

THE UNIVERSE AS PICTURED
IN
MILTON'S PARADISE LOST

TO

PROFESSOR E. CHARLTON BLACK,

Doctor of Laws (Glasgow University)

In proof of my high esteem for your character, and of my appreciation of your eminent services as an interpreter in the vast field of English Literature, permit me, my beloved colleague, to inscribe to you this brief and imperfect attempt to promote on the part of the public, and especially among young teachers not possessed of your equipment, a better understanding of the poem which many have called immortal, and of which William Ellery Channing writes, that of all monuments of human genius it is perhaps the noblest.   W. F. W.

CONTENTS

ERRATUM

On page 7, third line under "Appendix,"
and on page 74, first line, George H.
Himes should read John A. Himes.

FOREWORD

ALTHOUGH Copernicus had finished his life-work sixty-eight years before the birth of Milton, the traditional geocentric conception of the universe was the only one generally held and taught at the latter date. Newton was as yet unborn, Bacon's Novum Organon yet unwritten. Kepler, illustrious improver and promoter of the Copernican doctrine, was still engaged upon his astronomic problems; but even he to his dying day followed tradition so far as to believe in the existence of a solid sphere, two German miles in thickness, in which all the nonplanetary stars were immovably "fixed." Milton was twenty-five years of age when Galileo was obliged to make upon his knees his historic abjuration of doctrine at Rome. Eight years after this our poet was in Florence and visited Galileo, but, so far as known, without making profession of faith in the new heliocentric teaching. In that generation the mediæval conception of the world was far more familiar to the peoples of Europe than any later one is to-day. And it was wonderfully complete and satisfying to the reason. In it the world-whole had a known center, and this being the Earth, it was one whose centrality seemed ocularly demonstrated daily and nightly by the geocentric movements of the heavenly bodies. In this same conception the world-whole had also a known circumference within which all beings had their appropriate places. This completeness and harmony of cosmographic thought we have lost. To-day no astronomer can tell us what is the center, or what the circumference of the world in which we are living. No wonder that Hegel openly deplored the loss of a cosmology so true to appearances, so venerable in age, and so dignifying to Man as the chief of all creatures.

In Paradise Lost the poet has prefixed to each of the twelve books a so-called "Argument," in which he briefly states in plain and serviceable prose the contents of the ensuing division of the poem. We can but wish he had also prefixed to the entire work an equally clear account of the universe as it lay in his forecasting thought and as it was to find expression, here a little and there a little, in his rhythmic pages. In twenty lines he could no doubt have outlined his Heaven and Earth and Hell with a clearness and completeness now unattainable by the most painstaking interpreter. In the lack of such an authentic presentment we can only gather up the cosmographic allusions scattered through the twelve books and combine them as harmoniously as possible, remembering that they relate to the space-world viewed at three distant epochs: (1) a time prior to the creation of the present heavens and Earth; (2) a time after the creation of the present heavens and Earth, but before the establishment of the present order of unequal days and diverse seasons; and (3) the time since the establishment of the present order.

Fortunately, the universe of Paradise Lost is no novelty invented by the author for the purpose of heightening the charm of his epic. It is the universe of his teachers and of his time. Its motionless Earth and homocentric heavens are essentially the same that we find in Plato and Ptolemy, in Aquinas and Dante. For this very reason its mastery is all the more important and interesting to every person as yet unacquainted with it. The study has been deplorably neglected for more than a century, but there are signs of improvement in various quarters, and as an introduction thereto the English language has no masterpiece so admirably adapted as Paradise Lost. In proportion as the following pages shall assist younger readers to think Milton's thoughts after him, and to gain a realization of the beauty and glory of the world in which the stately epic moves, in that proportion will the desire and aim of the writer be fulfilled.

INTRODUCTION

THE geocentric world-view of ancient and mediæval thought has been so completely superseded by the Copernican, that beginners in the study of Dante and Milton, if unaided by instructors of rare qualification, become simply bewildered in their efforts to reproduce in imagination the localities and dramatic movements set before them in the masterpieces of these authors. One of the most eminent and experienced of English professors of literature, the late David Masson, well says, "To every edition of the Divina Commedia there ought to be prefixed a diagram, however vague and crude, of the cosmological scheme adopted in the poem, or invented for it." In his opinion, students of Milton equally need a diagram of the Miltonic universe. Accordingly, he prepared and published one with careful explanations of Milton's cosmological terms and references; and his example has been followed by Himes, Sprague, and Orchard. The striking lack of agreement, however, between these diagrams and explanations shows that if any one of them is true to Milton's thought, all the others must have misled the students to whom they were taught, and must be still misleading as

many readers as rest in them. That they
may be conveniently compared with each other,
and with the text of the poem, five are reproduced in an appendix to the present essay.

The first of the series, that of Professor
Masson, was the earliest in publication, and
it has met with more general approval than
any of the others. To the present writer,
however, each of the five seems defective in
more than one particular. The author of
each has assumed without warrant that both
Heaven and Hell must be given a definite
boundary and shape. In each both regions
are inclosed on every side. It is true that in
Dr. Orchard's picture Heaven is not roofed in,
but in his text he twice describes it as "a hemisphere," and copies Masson's diagram as correctly representing it. I cannot think this
to have been the poet's idea. Like Plato,
Milton thinks of Heaven as extending illimitably
above the starry sphere. As if to protest in
advance against any inclosing or shaping of
the heavenly world, he expressly warns his
reader not to attempt to conceive of it as in
any determinate form, "square or round"
(ii. 1048). In like manner, as Heaven is summitless so Hell is bottomless. It is true that
in the exercise of his poetic license, he once
speaks of a "bottom," and once of a "lowest
bottom," but elsewhere and more scripturally,
it is the "bottomless pit" (vi. 866). And for

this, one has given a profound reason. "Before the creation of Hell and Earth," says Chambers, following Masson, "Chaos occupied the whole lower half of Infinity"; consequently, as Hell's territory is simply the expropriated undermost part of the original domain of Chaos, according to ii. 1002, it cannot be a bounded and shut-in dungeon, but is in reality "the dark unbottomed, infinite Abyss"(ii, 405). So it should be represented in every picture of Milton's cosmology.

Against the diagram of Professor Himes two further faults might be charged. First, the panoplied angels falling from his Heaven-gate could never have landed in a Hell so far removed from the region directly beneath Heaven; and, second. he places Hell's gates in a perpendicular wall on a level with his supposed floor of the region, while in the poem these gates are "high in the fiery concave of the horrid roof" (ii, 643; compare 635, and 437).

Without further criticism of preceding interpretations, the effort will here be made to present in ten clear and simple paragraphs the essential features of Milton's universe. One cannot hope to harmonize to a nicety every detail, for the poet is often studiously vague, piling up incongruous terms in order the better to suggest the inexpressible, and to get the psychological effects of ideas ineffable. Especially are diagram lines and angles and measurements helpless and worse than helpless in the representation of beings and movements essentially superspatial and supertemporal. On the other hand, in the realm of the strictly finite, no poet has ever given us cleaner cut or more harmonious cosmical conceptions. One is filled with admiration when noting how preadjusted is environment to action in every successive scene set before us in the unfolding drama. Ages of patient thought had prepared the stage. How effectively we may see in part in Plato. Wonderful is that cosmic whole presented us in Plato's Republic. Wonderful its eight geocentric spheres revolving one within the other and together producing the ravishing Music of the Spheres. But in Milton's day, in view of post-Platonic astronomical problems, two additional spheres had been invented, the Crystalline, and the Primum Mobile. The Crystalline was believed to inclose the Earth-inclosing eight, and the Primum Mobile to inclose the thus resulting nine. So came to its completion the so-called Alphonsine cosmology in which Milton was instructed and which he taught to his pupils. Its universe was one in which his contemporaries were thoroughly at home and one which comes to some degree of expression in nearly every one of his poems. Chaucer and Spenser and Shakespeare had lived in it and beautified it; the Bible, as then in-

terpreted, had made it sacred.   Earth was the
divinely appointed center of the creature-world,
the focus of vision for all intelligences.   The
heavens declared the glory of God by revolving
around the home of man.   Whenever the
soul of a dying saint was summoned to heaven,
availing itself of the polar passage described
in iii, 528, it mounted first to the Earth-inclosing lunar sphere, then to the higher Earth-
inclosing sphere of Mercury, then to that of
Venus, then in its turn to that of the Sun,
Mars, Jupiter, Saturn; then on and up through
the sphere which bears the Fixed Stars; then
on and up through the Crystalline sphere;
then on and up through the Primum Mobile;
to and through a Celestial Gate which, immovably fixed high above all ranges of perish-
able creaturehood, gives entrance to the New
Jerusalem, the indescribably and unimaginably
glorious City of God (iii, 481ff.).

Such is the Universe which every new reader
of Paradise Lost must needs explore.[1]   We
call it Milton's, but in every essential it ante-
dates Milton by thousands of years.   He is
simply the last of the long line of great masters
who wrought upon it.   As he leaves it, it is
the consummate product of ages of constructive
scientific and poetic thinking.   As such it

---

[1] The oldest English setting forth of sixteenth-century cosmography
with which I am acquainted dates from 1549, and is found in the "Mono-
log Recreative" part of The Complaynte of Scotland, edited for the
Early English Texts Society by J. A. H. Murray.   See pp. 47ff.

should be studied, understood, appreciated; then taught to each new generation as one of the choicest treasures of the human race.

To aid the reader in connecting and readily understanding the offered theses two diagrams are prefixed, neither of which has before been published. Then to show how far the essential features of Milton's Universe antedate the age of Ptolemy, and even that of Plato, a third diagram is added, in which the world-view of the ancient Babylonians is presented. This last was published in the Journal of the Royal Asiatic Society of London, in the year 1908, and respecting it Professor Sayce, of Oxford University, wrote, "It entirely satisfies all requirements of the Babylonian inscriptions, which is not the case with any other that has hitherto been brought forward."

In tracing the history of this remarkably complete and harmonious world-view from age to age, down to the time of Milton, the student will find valuable aid in Dreyer's "Planetary Systems from Thales to Kepler." But Dreyer confines himself so strictly to European astronomers and cosmologists that, in the lack of recent English works of a more comprehensive character, it has been necessary to refer in the following pages with some frequency to writings of my own in this field, namely, to Earliest Cosmologies (New York, 1909), and Paradise Found: The Cradle of the Human

Race at the North Pole (Boston, 11th edition, 1898). This latter is temporarily out of print, but a twelfth edition, with literature to date, is in preparation. Meantime it is a gratifying sign of growing interest in these studies that in England Dr. Orchard's Astronomy of Milton's Paradise Lost has lately reached its second edition. No previous writer has presented this branch of our subject in a form so scholarly and attractive, and it is a pleasure to commend it to all readers of our poet.

The Universe Before the Creation of the Earth and Its Heavens

HEAVEN
CULMINATING
IN THE MOUNT AND THRONE OF GOD

Heaven-Gate

REALM OF CHAOS
AND OLD NIGHT

Hell-Gate

HELL, TERMINATING IN THE
BOTTOMLESS
PIT

23

The Universe After the Creation of the Earth and Its Heavens

HEAVEN
CULMINATING
IN THE MOUNT AND THRONE OF GOD

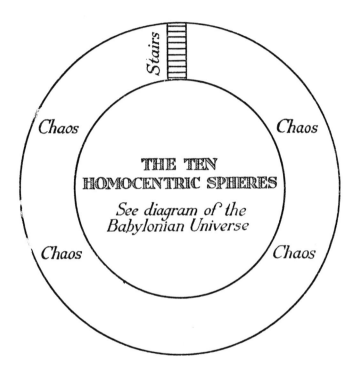

Stairs

Chaos   *Chaos*

**THE TEN
HOMOCENTRIC SPHERES**

*See diagram of the
Babylonian Universe*

Chaos   *Chaos*

**HELL, TERMINATING IN THE
BOTTOMLESS
PIT**

The Universe as Pictured by the Ancient Babylonians

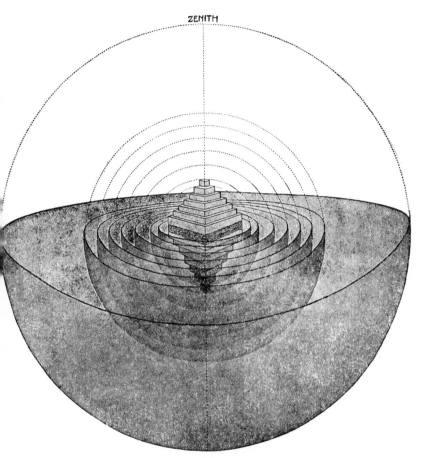

THE BABYLONIAN UNIVERSE

(The upper hemispheres cut away to show the interior)

The upright line is the polar axis of the heavens and earth. The two seven-staged pyramids represent the earth, the upper being the abode of living men, the under one the abode of the dead. The separating waters are the four seas. The seven inner homocentric globes are respectively the domains and special abodes of Sin, Shamash, Nabu, Ishtar, Nergal, Marduk, and Ninib, each being a "world-ruler" in his own planetary sphere. The outermost of the spheres, that of Anu and Ea, is the heaven of the fixed stars. In this world-view the spaces between the spheres widen rapidly at each remove from the Earth—so rapidly, in fact, that in a diagram of this size they cannot be represented otherwise than as above.

31

THE ESSENTIAL FEATURES OF THE UNIVERSE AS PICTURED IN PARADISE LOST

THE ESSENTIAL FEATURES OF THE UNIVERSE AS PICTURED IN PARADISE LOST

I. THE opening scenes of the poem bring to view three spatially distinct regions: (1) Heaven, the angelic world culminating in the Mount of God; (2) Hell, or the bottomless pit, a place prepared and held in readiness for the rebel angels; (3) an interlying region filled with Chaos, and of such enormous depth as to require nine days for a falling body to drop through it (vi. 671).

II. The limitless space in which the three regions coexist is represented as having a center and poles (i, 74); it must therefore be conceived of as orbicular, or spherelike. It will be found convenient to call it Milton's Macrocosm, in order to distinguish it from the later-created solar and stellar system which Milton sometimes calls "the World." To this Macrocosm he once seems to apply the term, "the hollow universal Orb" (vii, 257).

III. In the poetic descriptions the region of Chaos is always immediately above Hell, and immediately below Heaven; accordingly, viewed from the center of the spherelike whole, Heaven is ever at the zenith, and Hell at the nadir of the observer. Accordingly the polar axis of the sphere is absolutely perpendicular in position.

IV. Heaven is separated from the realm of Chaos by the ethereal sky. (i, 45), or by the Empyrean (vi, 833; x, 380). Being skylike, the Empyrean is most naturally conceived of as a hollow sphere, or world-shell, the lower half of which in like manner separates Hell from the realm of Chaos. Even Masson in the first of his diagrams represented the Empyrean, not as a hemispherical vault, but as a complete sphere (Life of Milton, vol. vi, p. 529).

V. The upper or northern, and the lower or southern, halves of the universe are counterparts with various answering features; for example, a Heaven-gate and a Hell-gate; a mount of God and a mount of Satan; summitless light and bottomless darkness. In the world-whole, however, the direction "downward" is not toward the mathematical center of the Earth (as invariably in Dante's world), but always toward a point in or below the lowest hell.

VI. The "gap" through which the rebel angels were driven out of Heaven is identical in position, and in function, with the elsewhere often mentioned Heaven-gate (vi, 861–879; ii, 990–997).

VII. Corresponding in purpose to the Heaven-gate above is the Hell-gate beneath, each giving in opposite directions the only available passage from the domain of Chaos to the space outside. By reason of their positions in the world-shell they can be passed through only in an upward or downward direction. The language of the poem implies that the Hell-gate is plumb-linearly[2] beneath the Gate of Heaven (x. 88–90; v. 253–270; vii. 131–135; ii. 884–889).

VIII. The new "world," created within the ancient realm of Chaos in the "six days" mentioned in Genesis, may conveniently be styled The Cosm, to distinguish it from the vaster Macrocosm which on every side incloses it. As represented by the poet, it consists of the ten homocentric spheres of mediæval astronomy with the "sedentary" or "steadfast" Earth as their center (vii, 192ff.). In all likelihood The Cosm is to be pictured in thought as homocentric with The Macrocosm, for this supposition is in harmony with the geocentric theories of the universe maintained by the ancients, and any other adjustment seems to destroy the symmetry of the total system.

IX. In the thirteenth stanza of his Hymn of the Nativity, Milton speaks of the "Ninefold harmony" of the "Crystal Spheres," and in Arcades, line 64, he mentions the "nine infolded spheres." These expressions seem to

---

[2] The reader must pardon the unfamiliar adverb derived from the plumb line, for no other term can express the sense with equal accuracy.

imply that his newly created world lacked the tenth of the Alphonsine world-shells, the so-called Primum Mobile. On the other hand, in one of his Latin poems, the *De Idea Platonica*, line 17, he speaks of the "Tenfold heaven" (Coeli decemplicis). Furthermore, in Paradise Lost (iii, 483, and 562) he expressly refers to the Primum Mobile (the "first," counting from heaven, but the tenth counting from the Earth). This apparent discrepancy as to the number of the geocentric heavens is probably to be explained on the theory that in Milton's thought the music of the spheres was produced by the motion of the divinely attuned *material* spheres, and that the tenth was soundless because by nature *immaterial*. Other thinkers before him had thus conceived of the outermost sphere as purely kinetic, and incessantly in action to maintain the revolutions of the material harmony-producing nine.

X. The center of the new creation was the Earth; which, in its original perfection, was a "terrestrial heaven danced round by other heavens" (ix, 103). The question whether this central orb itself revolved Raphael leaves unsettled (viii, 15ff., 70f.). Above it on every side was the firmament, which was simply an

> Expanse of liquid, pure,
> Transparent, elemental air, diffused
> In circuit to the uttermost convex
> Of this great round (vii, 264).

Above this transparent elemental air on every side were waters, the so-called "waters above the firmament." As these did not hide the stars from the view of men, they must be thought of as usually vaporized to the point of invisibility, though ever ready for recondensation and for descent in the form of rain or snow. Viewed from a distance, these super-aerial waters, being a complete Earth-inclosing hydrosphere, would be as present below the Earth as above it, and in this sense the Earth could be said to be

> Built on circumfluous waters calm, in wide
> Crystalline ocean (vii, 270).

The polar axis of the Earth was originally perpendicular to the plane of the Zodiac. As a consequence, all days were equal in length, and

Spring

Perpetual smiled on Earth with vernant flowers (x, 678).

At each pole the low sun daily "rounded the horizon," instead of rising and setting, the motion being from left to right at the northern pole, but from right to left at the southern. At both

> Day unbenighted shone (l, 681).

After the fall of man, however, by divine command, the angels "turned askance the poles," and in consequence the path of the sun was changed, days of unequal length produced, and the alternations of summer and winter. Tempests followed and all the discords of the natural world. From line 692, however, it would seem that in the poet's view these were "slow" changes, and not effected all at once.[3]

---

[3] This suggestion of Milton's as to the origin of unequal days and diverse seasons in a displacement of the Earth's poles is no fancy originating in his poetic mind. It is a remarkable fact that nearly every great thinker in the earliest period of Greek philosophy taught that in the world's beginning the axis of the Earth was perpendicular to the sun's orbit, and that its present inclination is due to some prehistoric change. Meager as are our extant fragments of the writings of Empedocles, Leukippos, Anaxagoras, Diogenes of Apollonia, and Archelaus, said fragments yield evidence that all of these pioneer astronomers held this view. See Dreyer, History of Planetary Systems from Thales to Kepler, 1906, pp. 26, 27, 28, 31, 33, 34. Dreyer also shows that the sphericity of the Earth was as well known to the ancient astronomers and their successors as it was to Columbus. Planetary Systems, pp. 20, 38, 39, 53, 55, 117, 158, 172, 192, 220, 223, 225, 227, 229, 239, 242, 243, 249, 250. For a diagram of the Earth as conceived of and described by Columbus, see Paradise Found, p. 307. In our day few are aware that he felt himself called upon to correct the error of those who maintained that the Earth is really a sphere.

SUBORDINATE QUESTIONS MORE OR LESS COSMOGRAPHICAL

SUBORDINATE QUESTIONS MORE OR LESS COSMOGRAPHICAL

To this point the recovery of the Miltonic Universe has not been difficult. All statements in the ten numbered paragraphs seem clearly set forth or implied in the poem. Moreover, with the resulting picture of Milton's world in mind, any reader of Paradise Lost can follow the rapidly succeeding movements of the Dramatis Personæ—celestial, terrestrial, and infernal—without losing at any time his spatial bearings. There remain, however, a few minor questions of a more or less cosmographical nature for whose solution the data presented in the text of the poem seem inadequate. To elicit fresh investigations a few of these may here be mentioned.

1. The Locality of Satan's Second Interview with Sin and Death.—When we ask where Satan is supposed to be at the time of his second interview with Sin and Death we encounter a peculiar textual difficulty. Just at the moment of the meeting Satan is represented as "now returned to Hell" (x, 346); and as being "near the foot" of the upright structure built by Sin and Death from Hell-gate to the level reached by the golden Heaven-

stair.   His location, therefore, as at or near
Hell-gate, seems doubly indicated; (1) he has
returned from Earth to his own infernal abode;
and (2) he is at the "foot" of a viaduct which
rises from that abode to the summit of the ten
homocentric heavens.   But, strangely enough,
some lines further on, as Satan is closing his
speech, he is evidently, not at the bottom,
but at the top of the bridge.   On it he pro-
poses to "descend" to Hell (1, 394); on it he
does "descend" (1, 414); furthermore, to reach
the terrestrial Paradise Sin and Death must
"descend" (1, 398); all three of them are "near
Heaven's door" (1, 389).   Has the poet in
closing the scene forgotten where he began it?
That seems incredible.   Have we evidence
here, then, of inadvertence on the part of
some one of the poet's numerous amanuenses?
This also seems incredible, for there is no one
word or clause, failure to catch which would
account for the discrepancy.

2. The Bridge, or Causey, Constructed
by Sin and Death.—The viaduct built "with
petrific mace" from Hell through Chaos to
the realms of light has been differently located,
and differently shaped, by different interpreters.
Of the five diagrams in our Appendix but one,
Dr. Orchard's, represents it.[4]   He starts the

---

[4] This paragraph was written a few days before Doctor Orchard published his new diagram, the one in which, in form and in position, The
Bridge is represented as by Masson.   To this our criticism does not
apply.

structure at a point in Hell quite removed
from the ninefold Gate, and carries its head
in as straight a line as is well possible to the
foot of the Heaven-stair.   Masson does not
picture it but tells us how it may be inserted
in his diagram.   He says: "The bridge not only
followed the track which Satan had taken
across Chaos, but it terminated, in adamantine
fastenings, exactly at the spot ('the selfsame
place') on the bare outside shell or Primum
Mobile of the Cosmos where Satan had alighted
after his toilsome flight; i. e. on its upper
boss, near the orifice where the Cosmos was
suspended from the Empyrean.   If the reader,
then, will take the diagram in the Introduction,
and draw with pen or pencil a curved line,
from the middle of what is there the arched
roof of Hell, upwards on the left hand into
the angle made by the equatorial line and the
circumference of the little circle representing
the Cosmos, that line will mark the track of
the bridge built by Sin and Death.   The some-
what obscure five lines 320–324 will then be
perfectly intelligible; for it will then be seen
how 'in little space the confines met of Empyrean Heaven, and of this World, and on the
left hand Hell with long reach interposed.'
But what are 'the three several ways' leading
'in sight to each of these three places'?   The
bridge itself is one of them, leading to Hell;
the mystic stair, or golden passage of communi-

cation, up from the orifice into the Empyrean, described at iii, 501–522, is another; and the downward shaft into the Cosmos from the same orifice right to Earth, described in the continuation of that passage (iii, 523–539), is the third."

Here then, in place of Orchard's essentially straight bridge, we have one curved from end to end. Moreover, the two differ as to the location of the foot of the structure, Orchard erroneously carrying it far to the left of Hellgate. Stopford Brooke, in his Milton Primer, page 87, agrees with Masson as to the location of the foot, but carries its head only to "the *base*" of the Cosm. Apparently, he agrees with Orchard, and differs from Masson, in making the structure rectilinear. The parallelism of the Bridge to the Heaven-stair, in its function, favors Brooke's interpretation, but the reading of the text in its present state at x, 312ff., clearly bars it out.[5]

3. The Quadrifurcate River of Eden, and the Quadriune River of Hell.—In the Biblical account of Eden, Gen. 2. 10, we read of a Paradisaic stream, which was "parted" and "became four" world-watering rivers. On

---

[5] In The Dial, of Chicago, March 7, 1915, under the caption, "Did Milton Nod?" I called attention to the textual difficulty in book ten, and to its necessary bearing upon our conception of the Bridge, asking at the same time for any suggestion that might be helpful. In response, an Iowa correspondent printed in the same organ, issue of March 18, a communication which I find difficult to understand, but to which I am glad to refer any reader in search of further light.

the other hand, in Paradise Lost, ii, 575, we
read of *four* infernal rivers, which *unite*, and
become one, as they together disgorge their
baleful streams into a burning lake.[6]   Does
Milton desire the reader to counterpose these
two pictures and so constitute a further inverted parallelism between the Upper and the
Underworld?

Probably not.   Had this been his wish, he
would naturally have made his Fountain by
the Tree of Life, ix, 73, one that sent four
streams to four opposing points of the com-
pass.   In iv, 433, he almost does this, yet not
quite.   It starts many questions to discover,
outside of the book of Genesis, such a four-
faced Fountain; and to find it in most of the
great mythologies of antiquity.   In not a few
it is regarded as the one headspring of all
the waters of the world.   It is clearly traceable
in the Rig Veda, in Homer's Iliad, in the
Puranas of India and Suttas of China.   In
his *Vorchristliche Unsterblichkeitslehre*, vol. ii,
p. 6, Wolfgang Menzel affirms that the four
infernal rivers of Greek mythology are antipodal
counterparts to the four Paradise rivers of the
Upperworld.   Dante teaches nearly the same
thing, for his one stream rising on the summit
of the terrestrial Paradise later feeds the four
rivers of Hell.

---

[6] Professor Himes's interpretation of the relation of the four infernal
rivers to Lethe is given in our Appendix.

On this topic the interested reader may find much curious and suggestive matter in Paradise Found, particularly in the chapter on "The Quadrifurcate River," pp. 250–261. See also Earliest Cosmologies, pp. 74, 98, 116, 190, 195, 206.

4. THE CIRCUMFLUOUS WATERS.—How Milton intended us to picture the "circumfluous waters in wide Crystalline ocean" (vii, 270), is a problem not easy of solution. Dr. Orchard, if I correctly understand him, describes them as a "Jasper Sea," annular in shape, perpetually in a horizontal motion around the northern pole of the ninth sphere, close to the foot of the Heaven-stair. So viewed, the waters are a circular river without head-spring or embouchment, like Lethe in Himes's diagram of the Infernal Rivers. What purpose such a river could there serve he does not explain, and it is hard to imagine any. Moreover, the statement that the Cosm was built "on" these circumfluous waters seems to bar out such an interpretation. Is it not more likely that Milton had in mind the "refluent Okeanos-river" of the Greeks, "which Aristotle describes as having its origin in the upper heavens, descending thence in rain upon the earth, feeding, as Hesiod, Homer, and Euripides said, all fountains and rivers, and every sea; then branching out into the rivers of the Underworld, to be returned fire-purged and sublimated

to the upper heavens, there to recommence its round"? (John O'Neill, "The Night of the Gods," vol. ii, p. 866.) The Avestan picture of the unitary water-circulation of the universe as the Iranians conceived it presents a most interesting parallel, as may be seen in Paradise Found, pages 251–254. Verity, in his edition of Milton, seems to make the ninth sphere consist of water ("a vast expanse of waters"), but says nothing as to the existence, direction or purpose of any "flow." The purpose of the so-conceived water-envelope above the eighth sphere is said by him to be "to protect the Earth from the 'evil influences' of Chaos; those 'fierce extremes' of temperature which might penetrate through the outside shell (the Primum Mobile), and 'distemper' the whole fabric of the universe did not this wall of water interpose (vii, 272–273)." Some of the mediæval writers assign the same regulative function, especially a cooling one, to what are called in the Bible "the waters above the firmament." As in Paradise Lost, according to Verity, the air extends all the way from the Earth to the Crystalline sphere; his identification of the waters above the firmament with a *sphere* of waters above the sphere of the Fixed Stars involves no inconsistency. It remains difficult, however, to understand how the Primum Mobile could apply to the ninth sphere the force necessary to give due rotary motion to it and to the eight inferior spheres in case the ninth was nothing more than a vast bubblelike globe of water. In any case Milton himself has not fully defined his thought on this point.

Right here it is interesting to note that in the "College Exercise," lines 34–52, a poem written in his nineteenth year, our poet recognizes with touches of rare beauty each of the four subcelestial, concentric Elemental Spheres of the ancient Greek tradition—those of "Fire, Air, Water and Earth"; and all of them in the orthodox order of their sequence, taking "Heaven's Door" as one's starting point. Inasmuch, however, as in line 41 he does not sharply separate the aqueous stratum from the aerial, it is difficult to say how far he would have us separate his subaerial waters from the superaerial, or waters above the firmament. This obscurity, it must be added, is by no means peculiar to Milton. The reader will find a remarkable array of conflicting interpretations of this elusive term, "firmament," set forth in Earliest Cosmologies, pp. 44, 45, footnote.

5. THE AXIAL OPENING THROUGH THE TEN SPHERES FOR THE PASSAGE OF THE ANGELS.— Some interpreters of Milton's universe have missed the true conception of the geocentric spheres by picturing at least nine of them as nothing more than imaginary divisions of empty

space.[7] They do not deny that the poet describes the outermost as a substantial, space-occupying world-shell, but they are fond of calling all the others defined "portions of transpicuous space." A sufficient refutation of this view seems to me to be found in the "Passage wide" mentioned in iii, 527ff. If the nine spheres are not conceived of as entities which occupy space, what call can there be for an open passage to serve as a free highway between Heaven and Earth? Furthermore, on this interpretation, no passage could be called "wide," for any passage, in any direction, on any side of the Earth, would be as wide as the whole interior diameter of the Primum Mobile. As far up as the eighth the spheres are, of course, transpicuous, since otherwise the stars would never be visible to men, but in the poet's thought they are ever present in their proper places and motions.[8] Milton's doctrine of the transmutability of body into spirit and of spirit into body (v, 407ff.) suggests caution in applying to the spheres the term "corporeal" or "material," but we are surely warranted in conceiving of them as not less real and space-occupying than are the ninefold gates of Hell, or the Archangel Michael

---

[7] See Verity, vol. i, p. 141. And yet on the preceding page, 140, he himself says of Milton's Earth, "It is *encased* by numerous *shells*."

[8] Dante does not hesitate to call even the ninth sphere a "*corpo.*" See the very valuable essay on "The Astronomy of Dante," in Edward Moore's "Studies in Dante," Third Series, 1903, p. 15.

and his panoplied host. Indeed, the conception here criticized is absolutely unthinkable. How can nine defined portions of the one transpicuous space move one within the other in the one unmoving transpicuous space that includes them all? In *vacuo* there can be no moving *vacua*.

The passage here provided for the angels is a wide opening at the upper pole of each of the ten geocentric globes (v. 269). Naturally, it cannot be elsewhere, for the spheres are revolving at different rates of speed, and any perforation not near the axial line, even if made, would instantly be closed by one or another of the whirling heavens. At the pole, and there only, can the opening remain open, and so afford a permanent passageway for the ascending and descending messengers of God (see Orchard's diagram). Gazing down the passage from the Heaven-gate, or the Heaven-stair, eyes of angelic range would survey, not successive portions of an Earth which was perpetually rolling over, but, on the contrary, the complete perpetually present northern hemisphere of an Earth as stable as the throne of the Almighty himself (v. 258ff.). Each Earth-inclosing sphere was transpicuous, for through them the stars adorning the eighth were visible to men.[9] At the same time each

---

[9] Aquinas, in a single sentence, expressly teaches us (1) the substantiality of these heavens, (2) their transpicuousness, and (3) the

was conceived of as a substantial shell-like creation, with strength to bear each its "officious lamp" (ix, 104). The invisible lunar sphere bore upon some part of its exterior surface the visible moon; the invisible Mercurial sphere the visible Mercury; the third sphere the dazzling Sun; the fourth, lovely Venus, and so on. Each of the inner eight had a distinctive light and color; each a distinctive rate of revolution; each a distinctive note in the diapason of the resulting "ninefold harmony." Small wonder that on his first view into such a divinely beautiful and musical revolving kaleidoscope of almost infinite dimensions, "wonder seized" the spirit malign (l. 552).

At this point the question may be raised whether in his flight precipitant down the polar passage Satan alighted on the sun we see, or upon the invisible Earth-inclosing "solar sphere" at some other point. Probably ninety-nine out of every hundred readers fail to remember that the interview with Uriel could have been elsewhere than on the visible sun. Most likely it was so viewed in the poet's mind, since the archangelic Regent of the sphere would naturally be interviewed in the most glorious of his palaces. Still, if one reads lines 588–590 carefully, and strongly emphasizes

proof that these qualities cannot be mutually exclusive: "*Sed quia corpus firmamenti etsi sit solidum, est tamen diaphanum quod lumen non impedit, ut patet per hoc quod lumen stellarum videmus non obstantibus mediis caelis,*" etc. (Summa, I, lxvi, 3).

the word "lucent," it becomes plain that the other interpretation is not ruled out.   Here, as everywhere in these studies, we cannot too painstakingly watch the important distinction between the Earth-inclosing sphere and the "lamp" of service which it bears.   (Compare "Earliest Cosmologies," pp. 101, 118, 199.)

6. The Cosmographical Location of Milton's Paradise.—For centuries the true site of the biblical Garden of Eden was persistently sought, not only by Jewish and Christian theologians, but also by explorers and travelers in various parts of the earth.   Extraordinary theories were proposed and defended.   More than two hundred years ago Bishop Hûet deplored the lack of certainty, and wrote: "Some have placed it in the third heaven, some in the fourth; some in the heaven of the moon, in the moon itself, on a mountain near the lunar heaven, in the middle region of the air, out of the earth, upon the earth, beneath the earth, in a place that is hidden and separated from man.   It has been placed under the northern pole, in Tartary, or in the place now occupied by the Caspian Sea.   Others have placed it in the extreme south, in Terra del Fuego; others in the Levant, or on the shores of the Ganges, or in the island of Ceylon. It has been placed in China, or in an inaccessible region beyond the Black Sea; by others in America, in Africa, and so on."   The dis-

cussion has continued to the present time, and it is interesting to learn from one of his letters that Livingstone was sustained in his tireless perambulations in the Dark Continent by the firm belief that if he could once reach the source of the Nile, he would stand upon the very site of the primeval Paradise.

Milton, like Dante, locates his Garden of Eden with great definiteness. It is remarkable, however, that the locality he indicates is about as far removed from that indicated by Dante as was anyway possible on the surface of the same Earth. Milton's is at the summit of an incomparably lofty mountain in Western Asia, more exactly on the northernmost frontier of Assyria (iv, 208ff.); Dante's, on the other hand, on the summit of an incomparably lofty mountain in the then unexplored South Pacific Ocean, exactly antipodal to Jerusalem (Purg. iv, 68; xxviii, 118–142). But these locations are geographic merely, not cosmographic. In other words, they leave us in each case uncertain as to the aboriginal, or even the later, zenith of the Terrestrial Paradise in the thought of the poet. As to Milton's conception, we learn from v, 258–260, that to Raphael, gazing down the polar passage through the ten revolving spheres, the Garden was distinctly visible; but as this was before man sinned and before the poles were turned askance, we can only infer that in the poet's mind the sacred

site was at that time in the northern hemisphere, and its zenith north of the celestial
equator in the eighth sphere.[10] Precisely at
the northern pole the Garden and its zenith
cannot then have been, for before Raphael's
interview with Adam was concluded the sun
was sinking toward its daily setting (vii, 98);
and, as we have seen, Milton well understood
that in his primal adjustment of the spheres
there could be no sunsets or sunrisings at
the poles of the earth (x, 689).

But while our poet leaves so much of uncer-
tainty with respect to the astronomic bearings
of his Paradise Mountain, he does not leave
us uninformed as to its destined translocation
into the deep sea. Among the things fore-
shown by Michael to Adam is the coming of
the Universal Deluge, and here the Archangel
adds:

"Then shall this Mount
Of Paradise by might of waves be moved
Out of his place, pushed by the horned flood,

---

[10] In reading Dante's grotesque suggestion in Inferno xxxiv, 121ff., one
wonders between which constellations of the eighth sphere the poet
imagined Lucifer to have passed in his headlong fall in line with Eden to
his fixed lodgment in the frozen center of the Earth. The poem gives
us no light upon the question, but it is some relief to know that its
author well understood the precession of the equinoxes and the necessary effect of the processional movement upon the zenith at every point
of the Earth's surface from century to century from the beginning to the
end of the thirty-six thousand years assigned by Ptolemy for the completion of the Magnus Annus (Purg. xi, 108; also i, 24; xxxiv, 1–7, with
notes of Castrogiovanni). Even the Southern Cross, here associated
with pristine humanity, settles nothing, for the astronomers assure us
that ages ago, and still long after the beginnings of human history, the
Southern Cross was visible in Siberia.

With all his verdure spoiled, and trees adrift,
Down the great river to the op'ning gulf,
And there take root, an island salt and bare,
The haunt of seals, and orcs, and sea-mews' clang;
To teach thee that God attributes to place
No sanctity, if none be thither brought
By men who there frequent, or therein dwell" (xi, 829).

What a subject for the pencil of a Gustave Doré! I can recall no parallel picture in Homer, Vergil, or Dante.

In Paradise Regained (iii. 251ff.), Milton locates with some definiteness the "exceeding high mountain" to which the devil conveyed our Lord for his third and crowning temptation; but while its summit, like that of the original Paradise Mountain, overlooked Assyria, he nowhere tells us that the two mountains are one and the same. On the contrary, he distinguishes them (Paradise Lost, xi, 381) and seems to picture the former as something almost, if not quite, spectral and supernatural (Paradise Regained, iv, 40–42). Of course he could hardly do otherwise, if from its top all the kingdoms of the Earth were to be surveyed.

But while our poet has not located the triumph of Jesus over the Tempter in the precise locality in which the Tempter triumphed over Eve and Adam, the luring poetic fitness of such a procedure is evident. And for centuries past the pilgrim to Jerusalem has been interested to find that local tradition at that chief of our holy places has identified the place of Man's Fall with the place of Man's Redemption by asserting that Primitive Eden was where the Holy City now stands. Little Gihon, he is told, is what now remains of the original Paradise river of that name. For further proof, the very tomb of Adam and Eve is pointed out to him. According to this teaching, the Garden of Eden and the Garden of Gethsemane consecrate the same soil and are framed in the same horizon. As late as 1862 an Englishman, W. Henderson, published in London a defense of this view, entitling his tractate, "Identity of the Scenes of Man's Creation, Fall, and Redemption" (see Paradise Found, pp. 231–233). One can but wonder what Dante would have said to such a point-blank inversion of his cosmographical teaching!

In the immemorially ancient mythical geography of the East Aryans we have a picture of the cradle of the human race which in several respects surpasses that presented by Milton. It includes one of the most striking of the biblical features, the Quadrifurcate River. It represents "Beautiful Meru" as the loftiest mountain in the world, so high that its head penetrates the lunar sphere, and there supports the throne-city of Indra, one of the gods. As it stands exactly at the north pole, the sun, moon, and all the stars move ma-

jestically round it in horizontal orbits from
left to right.   In its immovable position it is
always directly under the northern pole of all
the higher heavens, even to that of Great
Brahma, the highest and most powerful of all
the gods.   Here neither it, nor the sun, ever
really, or in appearance, goes *under* the Earth.
Its crest being a favorite resort of the gods,
the gardens and trees of life with which it
is adorned are more celestial than terrestrial.
From a higher-up heaven there descends upon
it a pure and life-giving stream which, descending thence in four opposite directions as four
world-rivers, waters the whole Earth.   Here
originated the first progenitors of the human
family, and from this polar center they pro-
ceeded to people the different *varshas* of the
habitable Earth.   See diagram and exposition
in Paradise Found, pp. 148–154.

Exactly under Beautiful Meru, the Mountain of the Gods, stands at the south pole its
inverted counterpart, the Mountain of the
Demons.   The one is inexpressibly bright and
glorious, the other the abode of darkness and
of all that is evil.   To pass from the upper
hemisphere to the lower one must pass the
River of Death.   In the oldest traceable beliefs
of the ancient Iranians also we find the same
conception of the figure of the Earth and
the same idea of the starting-point of the
earliest men (Paradise Found, p. 134).   Indeed,

according to Lenormant, the essential feature of this central Earth with antipodal polar mountains of incomparable magnitude, and of antagonistic spiritual significance, dates back to the earliest of all known Asiatic peoples, the Sumero-Babylonians (Paradise Found, p. 123n). The corresponding antipodality of Dante's Hell-cavity and Mount for scaling the Heavens leads one to wonder whether, even he had not read of the old Asiatic conception of the antipodal polar mountains, and whether he did not deliberately invert the demonian one in order to locate the embodying principle of evil as far as possible beneath the soil on which was committed the most diabolic of all historic, and of all conceivable deeds, the slaying of the one Earth-tenant "who was born and lived without sin" (Inf. xxxiv, 115). If such was really the origin of Dante's cosmos[11] in its central feature, it reflects all the greater credit

---

[11] A diagram of Dante's Earth and Hell is given in Paradise Found, page 307. Others showing his Heavens, Earth and Hell, have been published by many scholars. The lack of agreement in these is sometimes surprising. For example, in the one prefixed to Rossetti's "Shadow of Dante," The Rose of the Blessed in the Heaven of Heavens is in the zenith of Jerusalem, while in the Figura Universale designed by Duke Caetani di Sermoneta, and reproduced in Dinsmore's "Aids to the Study of Dante," the same Rose is placed at the opposite pole of the Empyrean, and thus at a distance equal to the diameter of the total universe. For comparative study, see diagrams in "Studies in Dante," by Edward Moore, Third Series, Oxford, 1903; "Dante," by Edward G. Gardner, London, 1900; Paget Toynbee's "Dictionary of Dante," Oxford, 1898; "The Divine Comedy of Dante. Translated into English Verse, by John A. Wilstach," Boston, 1888; "Dante's Divine Comedy." A commentary by Denton J. Snider, 2 vols., 1893, and others.

upon his genius; for by this felicitous recon-
struction of the Earth of the ancients he at
once and forever delocalized the Divine Pres-
ence, and reduced to a vanishing point in
space and power the Malign Spirit which in
all preceding ages had shadowed the thought
and the lives of men.

A PRIME REQUISITE IN STUDIES
LIKE THE PRESENT

A PRIME REQUISITE IN STUDIES
LIKE THE PRESENT

"All outward vision yields to that within,
  Whereof nor creed nor canon holds the key."

Would one gain a correct view of the universe as pictured in any literary masterpiece the first requisite is a willingness, or, rather, an eager readiness, to *repicture* it in thought according to the data supplied by the author. Many fail to attain the desired end because they fail to exercise their imagination upon the problem. Especially do they fail when they neglect to think out the implications of a suggested cosmical feature or adjustment that is unfamiliar. When Milton suggests that before the fall of man the Earth's axis was not inclined as now, but was perpendicular to the plane of the sun's orbit, the reader should at once imagine himself on such an Earth and proceed to inquire into the extent of its unlikeness to the Earth we know. A moment's careful thought will, of course, convince him that at both poles of such an upright sphere the sun would always be visible on the horizon, and that in the lower latitudes all days and nights would be equal. Of course, too, there could be no alternation of summer's heat and winter's cold. Milton takes pains to tell us this much; but if we take time to think through the implications of the suggested cosmical adjustment more fully, we quickly make further discoveries. We find that owing to the refraction of the sunbeams by the atmosphere the lighted side of the supposed Earth would always be several degrees more than half of the total surface, and the unlighted side several degrees less than half. Accordingly, the sun would always be visible, not merely at the poles, but also several degrees beyond each pole. As a consequence, there would be at each pole a considerable area where night and its stars could never come. Stranger yet, we would find that if in one of these illuminated circumpolar areas two astronomers, A and B, were stationed two miles apart, with the pole exactly between them, and were to make a solar observation at the same instant, A dating his May 31, 11 P. M., and B his June 1, 11 A. M., the two dates would be equally correct. Surely, discoveries like these amply repay the slight effort of thought needed for their making.

Myopic interpreters of the Odyssey, possessed of no imagination, have for centuries tried to find Homer's world within the narrow limits of Hellas and the Levant. So doing, they have not only done violence to a multitude of passages in detail, but have even missed the author's prime claim upon the attention of moderns. Worse than that, being instructors of the young, they have been blind leaders of the blind in all that they have written touching the figure of Homer's Earth, and the Earth of Homer's contemporaries.[12]

The Maha-Bharata is the great epic of India, one of the greatest in the world. Its culminating scene, the ascension of Yudhish-thira into the heaven of Indra, is at the summit of Mount Meru, the incomparably lofty and glorious Paradise Mount at the north pole. But for this reason no reader who has not exercised his imagination upon the heaven of Indra, and upon the mythical relations of this Mount to the Varshas of the Earth on the one hand, and to the heavens above Indra's on the other, can possibly appreciate the significance of the time and place of this ascension, and the congruence of the epic incidents and speeches leading up thereto.

But Milton and the other epic-writers are not the only persons to make upon the reader demands of this kind. The scientist, not less than the student of literature has need of a constructive space-measuring and space-filling imagination. An ancient Greek cosmologist tells us that at the beginning of the world one

---

[12] For ample justification of the above statement, see Paradise Found, pp. 117–122, 328–361, 467–487. Also "Earliest Cosmologies," pp. 70–78, 157–191.

terrestrial day was equal to ten of our present
months. Had he said twelve months instead
of ten, he would have simplified his challenge
to our thought, and perhaps made it more
effective. In that case he would at once have
started us upon the inquiry as to the effects
of such a Year-day upon our sunrises and
sunsets. And here, again, but little thought
would be required to show us that to an observer at the pole under the supposed con-
ditions, the inclination of the Earth's axis
remaining as at present, sunrise would no
longer be in a spiral, as now, but would be in
an apparently straight line directly up from
the horizon toward the zenith; only so slow
that at the end of three months the sun would
have attained an altitude of but twenty-three
and a half degrees. Then—portentous sign—
it would stop, and for the next three months
slowly sink along the line of its rising, and
then disappear, to rise and set in the same
deliberate and apparently futile manner at
the opposite pole.[13]

Mental exercises of the kind just indulged
in are not to be lightly esteemed and dismissed
as merely entertaining; they often prove of
highest value. The great astronomers of history would never have made the advances with
which they have enriched the world had they

[13] For other anomalous experiences possible only in the circumpolar
regions, see Earliest Cosmologies, pp. 124ff.

not possessed and cultivated this faculty of
seeing beyond the immediately visible, and of
making themselves thoroughly at home in
conceived-of environments utterly unfamiliar.
And it may be added that this Greek reminder
of the relativity of our most common chrono-
metric units, the day and the year, prepares
one in a unique manner for a readier grasp
of many a detail in the teachings of the ancients relative to the World Periods, or Ages,
into which Creation's lifetime was by them
divided, and in which, in one ethnic form or
another, in one sæculum or another, about
every process in nature known to us as normal is held to be precisely the reverse of what
once was, or in some coming age will be the
normal. For the Babylonian, Buddhist, Egyp-
tian, Greek and Roman, Jewish, Mohammedan,
and Zoroastrian ideas on these mundane
recurrences, see "Encyclopædia of Religion and
Ethics," vol. i, pp. 183–290. Here the time-
world and the space-world are curiously com-
bined, and the history of human thought
respecting them illustrated in a manner which
neither science alone, nor literature alone,
could equal. And, strange to say, the latest
cosmic speculations of our astronomers and
physicists, with their alternating world-periods
of Evolution and Dissolution, seem little more
than revised editions of prehistoric teachings
touching the æonian life of the world.

APPENDIX
(See Reverse)

The Diagrams here given first appeared in the following publications, to wit:

No. I in the Bibliographical, Biographical, and Expository Introduction to Masson's three-volumed Library edition of Milton's Poetical Works, London, 1874.

Nos. II and VII in Study of Paradise Lost, by Professor John Andrew Himes, Philadelphia, 1878.

Nos. III and IV in Milton's Paradise Lost, Books First and Second, with Introduction, Notes, and Diagrams. By Homer B. Sprague, Ph.D., Boston, 1879.

No. V in The Astronomy of Milton's Paradise Lost, by Thomas N. Orchard, M.D., 2d edition, London, 1913.

Masson reprinted his with a slightly modified text in his Life of John Milton, Vol. VI, pp. 518–557.

Himes reprinted his in the slightly modified form given at the bottom of this page, in an edition of Paradise Lost issued by him in the year 1898. It is here reproduced with the courteous consent of the author and by arrangement with The American Book Company, his publishers.

Orchard's modification of No. V was given to the public in April, 1915, and is here reproduced by permission.

All of the above works have rendered valuable service, and may still be used with profit by students and teachers.

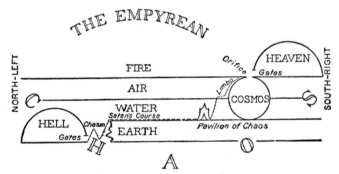

HIMES'S REVISED DIAGRAM OF MILTON'S UNIVERSE

72

I. MILTON'S UNIVERSE AS INTERPRE-
TED BY DAVID MASSON

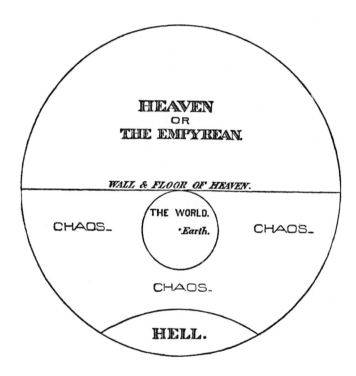

II. MILTON'S UNIVERSE AS INTERPRETED BY GEORGE H. HIMES

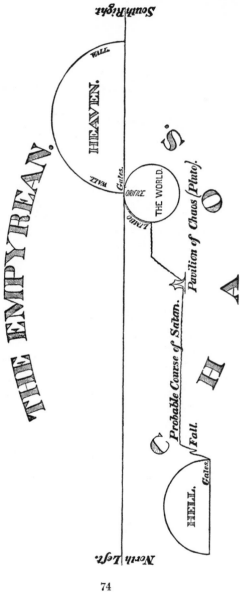

III. MILTON'S UNIVERSE AS INTER-PRETED BY HOMER B. SPRAGUE

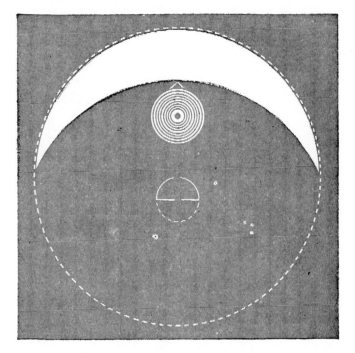

VERTICAL SECTION,
Showing (conjecturally) Milton's cosmography,—the Empyreal Heavens, our Starry Universe, Hell, and Chaos.

IV. AN ALTERNATIVE INTERPRETATION BY HOMER B. SPRAGUE

VERTICAL SECTION
(Sprague thinks this "perhaps more satisfactory" than the preceding.)

V. MILTON'S UNIVERSE AS INTERPRETED BY THOMAS N. ORCHARD

Diagram as published in 1913.

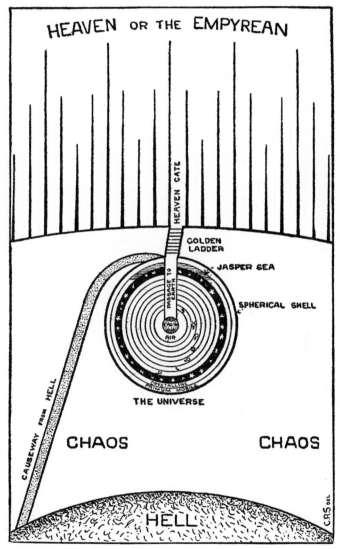

VI. MILTON'S UNIVERSE AS INTERPRETED BY THOMAS N. ORCHARD

Diagram as modified in 1915.

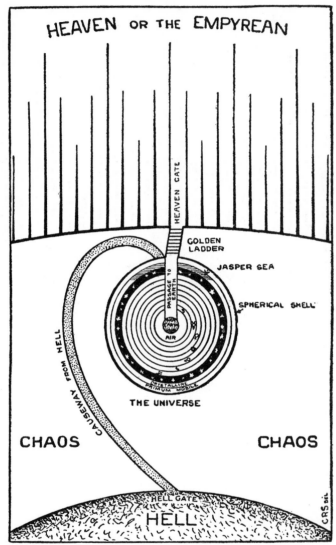

VII. "THIRD CIRCLE" OF MILTON'S HELL, ACCORDING TO HIMES

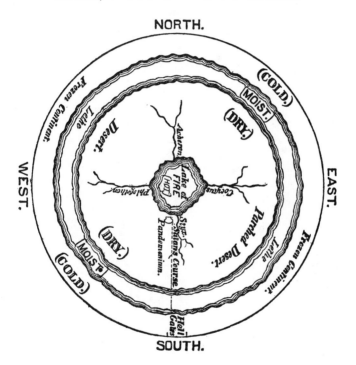

NORTH.

WEST.

EAST.

SOUTH.

INDEX OF NAMES